Presentation Page

Presented to

_____

Presented by

_____

Great and Precious Promises

For Singers and Musicians

Music and the Word Ministries

Published by Music And The Word Ministries
419 Dahlia Drive
Brentwood, TN 37027

Printed in the United States of America.
ISBN # 1-4158-2817-2
First Printing, August 2004
Second Printing November 2004

ISBN 1-4158-2817-2

9 781415 828175

For just as rain and snow fall from heaven,
and do not return there without saturating the earth,
and making it germinate and sprout,
and providing seed to sow and food to eat,
so My word that comes from My mouth
will not return to Me empty,
but it will accomplish what I please,
and will prosper in what I send it [to do]."

Isaiah 55:10-11

Table of Contents

What the Bible says about . . .

God wants you to . . .

Introduction

SINGERS AND MUSICIANS are very important to God. He created you and gave you talent and ability, and you have great potential residing within you. If you have accepted Jesus as Lord and Savior, you are an essential part of God's plan. It is God's clear intention that you fulfill your purpose as a member of His body and reach your full potential.

The dictionary defines potential this way: "that which has hidden or dormant power." It is God's deep desire that you receive and believe His Word and release the full power of the Holy Spirit residing in you.

The root word for potential is "potent," meaning "powerful, convincing." God desires for His singers, musicians, and worship leaders to be powerful and convincing proclamation tools on the earth. As you combine your God-given talent and carefully-developed skill with a full understanding of your purpose in

God's kingdom, you will become a more powerful and convincing voice. You will release your full potential and fulfill God's purpose for singers and musicians.

Your Pathway to Potential has four stepping-stones that are easy to remember:

Presence, Promises, Purpose, Process >>> Potential

The journey to releasing your full potential must start in God's **presence**. You have to spend time with God and really know Him in order to receive and believe His **promises** (John 15:7).

God inspired others to write down those promises in the Bible for you and me. As you read and hear God's Word, you receive revelation of His nature, His character, and His will for you. That's how your faith grows—by hearing the Word of God. And as you believe His Word, God's promises will help you identify and understand God's **purpose** for your life as a singer, musician, and worship leader.

The next step requires that you put your faith into action as you navigate the **process** of life—that "series of continuous actions and changes" that we all know so well. The process of life is seldom easy, but it is required to release the **potential**—the hidden power—that God has placed inside of you.

God never creates anything without a purpose in mind. And He created you with clear "intent, aim, design" a clear purpose:

To precede and proclaim His presence, His power, and His Word; preparing God's people to receive Him. (1 Chronicles 15:25-28)

To lead God's people as they celebrate, thank, and praise Him. (1 Chronicles 16:4 NAS)

The singers, musicians, and worship leaders under King Solomon provided a great example of musicians who understood their purpose and released their potential. When they became "as one" (harmonically and with unified purpose) during the dedication of the temple, God responded mightily:

"...the temple, the LORD's temple, was filled with a cloud. And because of the cloud, the priests were not able to continue ministering, for the glory of the LORD filled God's temple." 2 Chronicles 5:13-14

These musicians applied all their skill and talent to the purpose they were given in serving the Lord, and they saw God intervene in the lives of His people.

That is still God's desire today. As you fulfill His **purpose** through a deeper understanding of God's **promises** for you, you will be on the pathway to true freedom as a singer and musician. Then you will see that life's **process**—all the ups and downs—simply serves to ignite the fuel of God's Word and release the **potential** that He has already placed in you.

Circumstances, doubts, and fears cannot deter the man or woman who walks according to God's Word. Unbelief must flee in the face of God's relentless and unchanging promises.

Those promises are yours, if you will receive and believe them. You are very important to Him.

Stan Moser
Music and the Word Ministries

Presence

Immediate vicinity of something existing now,
not absent

Promise

Assurance, pledge, confidence
to do or not do something

Purpose

Aim, intent, design or object

Process

Series of continuous actions and changes

Potential

That which has hidden or dormant power
(Potent: powerful, convincing)

Ready, Willing and Able

GREAT AND PRECIOUS PROMISES For Singers And Musicians is designed to introduce you to some very simple principles that will help you as a singer, musician, and worship leader. Principles and godly instruction are always good, but good principles or great ideas are only valuable when they can be applied to real life.

Principles are good, but what we really need is God's presence.

A few years ago, in the midst of an amazing encounter one morning, the Lord led me to Luke 10. I was already familiar with the story of the Seventy Disciples that Jesus appointed in that passage of Scripture, but I soon realized that the Lord led me there for a very specific reason.

As I studied this passage, I began to realize that this group of people is a great example for all singers, musicians, and worship leaders. If you will look at their story closely, you will find that the Seventy revealed <u>four qualifications for service</u> that set them apart from the crowd. And God requires the same qualifications today for those He uses in ministry.

The Seventy weren't apostles or priests or kings. They were ordinary people just like you. The Bible doesn't name even one of the Seventy. They were just a part of the crowd, but God had a very important job for them to do. Their obedience to God's direction for their lives would have a major impact on His kingdom.

Time Well Spent

It's not hard to imagine Jesus being surrounded by a large crowd of people wherever He went publicly. After all, He was the Way, the Truth, and the Life. His miracles were well known, and people were always in need.

The Seventy were probably there for a variety of reasons, but they were there. Spending time in God's presence is the first qualification for service:

<u>God uses ordinary people who choose to spend time in His presence.</u>

If you are struggling today, wondering why your talent is overlooked or underused, I encourage you to set aside your feelings and questions and spend time in His presence. God made you and blessed you with talent and abilities. He knows where you are, and He knows your heart's desire. The most important step in unlocking your potential will always be spending time in His presence.

(Jesus said) If you remain in Me and My words remain in you, ask whatever you want and it will be done for you. My Father is glorified by this: that you produce much fruit and prove to be My disciples. John 15:7-8

Count the Cost
The story of the Seventy actually starts in Luke 9. That's when Jesus' ministry took a major turn:

"Now it came to pass, when the time had come for Him to be received up, that He steadfastly set His face to go to Jerusalem," Luke 9:51 (NKJV)

Until this time, Jesus had been setting the stage for His triumphant moment on the cross at Calvary (Colossians 2:15). The teachings, the healings, and the deliverances were done with one goal in mind: He was the Lamb who would be slain to take away the sins of mankind. There had always been a cross in His future, and the time had come for that climatic moment.

Jesus knew that the road He was about to travel was the most difficult one any man had ever known. Throughout all biblical history, the sacrifice of flesh and blood was required to atone for the sins of man. Those sacrificial lambs didn't know where they were headed and the price that they would pay. Jesus knew that the cross would cost Him everything. But the time had come—the Living Sacrifice had to be made.

"Behold! The Lamb of God who takes away the sin of the world!" John 1:29 (NKJV)

As Jesus made clear His plans to go to the cross, many of His followers declared their desire to go with Him, no matter what. Jesus responded by teaching them about the cost of discipleship. Following Jesus required total dedication then and now. Jesus makes it clear that there is no room for double-mindedness:

But Jesus said to him, "No one who puts his hand to the plow and looks back is fit for the kingdom of God." Luke 9:62

After uttering those words, Jesus appointed seventy ordinary people from the crowd for a very special mission—the same mission that God offers to singers, musicians, and worship leaders just like you today:

After this, the Lord appointed 70 others, and He sent them ahead of Him in pairs to every town and place where He Himself was about to go. Luke 10:1

The mission for the Seventy started in the presence of the Lord. They had believed and received His promises, and now Jesus was about to show them their purpose. Their willingness to go with Jesus in spite of the cost to them personally was their second qualification for service:

<u>God uses ordinary people who are willing to pay the cost necessary to fulfill their purpose in God's kingdom.</u>

Trust and Obey
The Seventy were about to be sent on the journey of a lifetime. They were about to be thrust into the process of a God-sized assignment and release the potential that had been dormant inside them their whole lives.

The Seventy were chosen to use their talents and abilities to proclaim the coming presence of the Messiah! Jesus sent them out into every city and place where He was about to go. They preceded and proclaimed the power, the presence, and the Word of God to people who needed a Savior.

That's the same purpose God has in mind for singers, musicians, and worship leaders today:

To precede and proclaim the power, presence, and Word of God; to prepare the hearts of the people to receive Him.

That mission and God's method haven't changed. The Lord still sends ordinary people to precede Him throughout the earth as He advances His kingdom. God still uses devoted people who spend time in His presence and are willing to respond to His direction.

The Seventy were given specific instructions about provisions, associations, locations, and how they were to respond in difficult situations. Jesus told them where to go, to trust Him for provision, to settle in the place He provided along the way, and how to overcome the rejection that they would encounter as they fulfilled their purpose.

Evidently, they understood and fulfilled their

mission according to His instruction. That is the third qualification for service:

<u>God uses ordinary people who are willing to do God's work, God's way, in the places God sends them.</u>

For singers, musicians, and worship leaders, God's direction is very clear in Scripture. It is important to develop your skills and talent to perform with precision and in harmony with those around you. But you must never let a situation that is less than perfect keep you from fulfilling your purpose!

The people in front of you are His people. They are in desperate need of a touch from the Savior, and you have been given the opportunity to prepare them for His glorious presence. They will hear and see you on the platform, but they really came to hear and see the King of kings. He is the only one who can intervene in their lives. Jesus is the Exalted One. Everything you do must point those precious people to Him.

If they leave the assembly without encountering the One who changes everything, you have come up short no matter how good you looked or sounded. While you must strive for perfection in your efforts, never lose track of your purpose. The Seventy remained true to Jesus' instructions and lives were changed:

The Seventy returned with joy, saying, "Lord, even the demons submit to us in Your name." Luke 10:17

The Seventy obeyed God—did things His way in the places He alone sent them—and they were filled with joy. They saw amazing results, and you can too!

The Heart of Worship—It's All About Him

Jesus responded to the Seventy and let them know that He was with them the whole time, and that greater accomplishments were on the way:

He said to them, "I watched Satan fall from heaven like a lightning flash. Look, I have given you the authority to trample on snakes and scorpions and over all the power of the enemy; nothing will ever harm you. Luke 10:18-19

God will be with you when you serve as well. Everything you do as His singer, musician, and worship leader that leads people to Jesus is accomplished through the Holy Spirit who dwells with you and within you. He is always present to lead submitted believers in the best and most difficult circumstances.

Then Jesus encouraged them not to be too impressed

with themselves or their abilities, but to honor Him with their worship and appreciation instead. That is the fourth qualification for service:

<u>God uses ordinary people who never glory in the adulation of the moment, but who recognize that they are being used by the One whom they will serve throughout eternity.</u>

However, don't rejoice that the spirits submit to you, but rejoice that your names are written in heaven."
Luke 10:20

Can you see the picture here for singers, musicians, and worship leaders? The applause of man doesn't matter. Your picture on the front of a CD doesn't matter. What matters is that God Himself sent you, you responded, and His kingdom was advanced. Holy is the Lord! All glory and honor belong to Him!

Four Qualifications for Service
You don't have to be a Bible scholar or a seminary graduate to serve God and see His hand at work. He has been using ordinary people just like the Seventy and you and me for a long time. The 'wise and prudent' sometimes sit and debate while God is clearly speaking.

Jesus is looking for 'babes' to glorify Him by fulfilling His purpose in their lives.

In that same hour He rejoiced in the Holy Spirit and said, "I praise You, Father, Lord of heaven and earth, because You have hidden these things from the wise and the learned and have revealed them to infants. Yes, Father, because this was Your good pleasure. Luke 10:21

That prayer is for you as you understand and act upon these <u>four qualifications for service:</u>

- God uses ordinary people who choose to spend time in His presence.

- God uses ordinary people who are willing to pay the cost necessary to fulfill their purpose in God's kingdom.

- God uses ordinary people who are willing to do God's work, God's way, in the places God sends them.

- God uses ordinary people who never glory in the adulation of the moment, but who recognize that they are being used by the One whom they will serve throughout eternity.

Encouraging Words

The story of the Seventy Disciples should be a great encouragement for singers, musicians, and worship leaders:

- God has given you talent and ability, and His purpose is clear: to precede and proclaim the power, presence, and Word of God; preparing the hearts of the people to receive Him.

- God wants you to develop the talent He has given you. He wants you to be a good steward of all your gifts. And He wants you to employ all the skill you can develop.

- God has uniquely positioned you where you are. You can fulfill your purpose and release all the potential within you in the place He has given you to serve. When God, and God alone, is ready to move you to a new location, He will make that abundantly clear. As you serve, you must do things His way, in the place He has set aside for you.

You already know that you will encounter rejection along the way. That's just part of the process of life for singers, musicians, and worship leaders. But God has shown you how to respond! If you are doing God's work, God's way, in the place that He has planted you, you can be confident that any such rejection rests on God's very broad shoulders, not your own. Now that is freedom!

Many who sing and play on the church platform get caught up in the praise they receive. When the Seventy seemed to face that same trap, Jesus gave them a way to overcome that obstacle as well. He reminded them that being used by God to impact people was just part of His plan. God alone deserves the glory as He works through you. There really is a dormant, hidden power that lies within you. You have great potential.

Principles are good, but what you really need is His presence.

Just like the Seventy, your journey must begin in His presence. You can believe the promises of God because you know the One who has promised. He alone will reveal your purpose. Life's process will become the fuel that ignites God's Word within you and releases your potential. That's what happened in

Luke 10 for seventy ordinary people, and that's what God wants to do in your life.

No matter where you are in life, God can use you. Circumstances and distractions will not deter the man or woman who submits wholly to God's mighty hand of grace. The Seventy experienced rejection and temptation, and so will you. Every step of faith requires a fight of faith, but God has made a way for you in every situation.

God wants you to fulfill your purpose as His singer and musician. Raise your voice of proclamation in the assembly. Sing and make melody in your heart unto the Lord. He is a good God! He alone is worthy of your praise. You were created for worship, and as you lead God's people to the very throne of grace, you will fulfill your purpose.

He has indeed given you everything you need for life and godliness according to His great and precious promises. You can count on it.

The Pathway to Potential

GOD'S PRESENCE

---

*Enter His gates with thanksgiving
and His courts with praise.
Give thanks to Him and praise His name.
Psalms 100:4*

Every journey has a beginning. From Abraham to Moses, through the gospels of Matthew, Mark, Luke, and John, and throughout the letters of the Apostle Paul, we see evidence of lives that were changed dramatically through a personal encounter with God. If you are a Christian, Jesus, the Living Word, drew you to Himself and changed your life forever as well.

The Bible is filled with the great and precious promises of God. His Word is a real, tangible expression of His love and provides hope for His people. But, just like any other relationship in this life, without a personal encounter with the One who promised, the promises are hard to believe and receive.

No matter what comes your way in this life, you can depend on the Lord. He is the One through whom, by whom, and for whom all things were created and all things hold together. He is God, the great I Am. He is the One who provides, delivers, defends and protects. He is your All in All. There is truly no one else like Him.

In His presence, you will find hope. You will find peace. You will find rest. And just like all great Bible heros, that's where your journey really begins. That's the place you have to go whenever God's promises are seemingly overwhelmed by life's process.

When you lead God's people in worship, you are making a place where God Himself is enthroned. God's singers and musicians are called to lead His people to that same place where they can encounter His glorious presence afresh. As you use the talent and ability that God has given you to draw others to that place of meeting, you can be assured of His pleasure.

If you haven't been in His presence recently, now is a good time to go. Lay aside the distractions and encumbrances of life for even a few minutes. God created you for His presence. He loves you with a never-ending love, and He wants to use you for His glory like never before.

It all begins in God's Presence.

He who dwells in the secret place of the Most High shall abide under the shadow of the Almighty. I will say of the LORD, "He is my refuge and my fortress; My God, in Him I will trust."

Psalm 91:1 (NKJV)

Be still, and know that I am God; I will be exalted among the nations, I will be exalted in the earth! Be still and know that I am God.

Psalm 46:10 (NKJV)

You reveal the path of life to me; in Your presence is abundant joy; in Your right hand are eternal pleasures.

Psalm 16:11

Surely the righteous shall give thanks to Your name; the upright shall dwell in Your presence.

Psalm 140:13 (NKJV)

No one will be able to stand against you as long as you live. I will be with you, just as I was with Moses. I will not leave you or forsake you.

Joshua 1:5

The Lord is a refuge for the oppressed, a refuge in times of trouble.

Psalm 9:9

Even when I go through the darkest valley, I fear [no] danger, for You are with me; Your rod and Your staff—they comfort me.

Psalm 23:4

"I am the vine; you are the branches. The one who remains in Me and I in him produces much fruit, because you can do nothing without Me. If you remain in Me and My words remain in you, ask whatever you want and it will be done for you.

John 15:5,7

GOD'S PROMISES

For every one of God's promises is "Yes" in Him.
Therefore the "Amen" is also through Him
for God's glory through us.
2 Corinthians 1:20

Everywhere you look these days, someone is promising you something. There are products that promise to make you thinner, smarter, richer, younger, and better looking. There are products that promise you security, success and even serenity. And these promises are often brought to you by well-known, talented, and credible people. Just pick up the phone and call absolutely free. All things are possible.

The Bible is also filled with great and precious promises. It is filled with assurances of hope, love, destiny, eternity, prosperity, purpose, security, and all the blessings we desperately long to receive. And these promises are brought to you by the One who is from the beginning the One who created all things—the only One who is worthy of all praise, glory, and adoration.

God's promises have stood the test of time, and yet, time is part of the problem we have with receiving and believing His promises. We simply don't take the time to know the One who promised, to meditate on what He has promised, and to wait on His promises to be fulfilled.

We must abide in Him and allow His words to abide in us, and that takes time and attention. There is an all-out battle for your time and attention being waged every day. With so many other voices and images assaulting our minds, there has never been a more crucial time to focus on God's promises. It takes discipline to turn off the television and the computer, and put away the newspapers and magazines.

However, the diligent effort to put God's Word first in these days does produce a guaranteed result. You will find peace, wisdom, renewed vitality, security and success there. Everything you need for life and godliness can be found in His great and precious promises.

God is not a man that He should lie. He is the same yesterday, today, and forever. The great I Am is promising life and life more abundantly. Just pick up His Word and receive, absolutely free of charge. He who promised is indeed faithful.

———————

For His divine power has given us everything required for life and godliness, through the knowledge of Him who called us by His own glory and goodness. By these He has given us very great and precious promises, so that through them you may share in the divine nature, escaping the corruption that is in the world because of evil desires.

2 Peter 1:3-4

God is not a man who lies, or a son of man who changes His mind. Does He speak and not act, or promise and not fulfill?

Numbers 23:19

In Him you also, when you heard the word of truth, the gospel of your salvation—in Him when you believed—were sealed with the promised Holy Spirit.

Ephesians 1:13

Let us hold on to the confession of our hope without wavering, for He who promised is faithful.

Hebrews 10:23

A thief comes only to steal and to kill and to destroy. I have come that they may have life and have it in abundance.

John 10:10

Bless the LORD, O my soul; and all that is within me, bless His holy name! Bless the LORD, O my soul, and forget not all His benefits: Who forgives all your iniquities, Who heals all your diseases, Who redeems your life from destruction, Who crowns you with lovingkindness and tender mercies, Who satisfies your mouth with good things, so that your youth is renewed like the eagle's.

Psalm 103:1-5 (NKJV)

Jesus Christ is the same yesterday, today, and forever.

Hebrews 13:8

Lord, Your word is forever; it is firmly fixed in heaven. Your faithfulness is for all generations; You established the earth, and it stands firm.

Psalm 119:89-90

Now we want each of you to demonstrate the same diligence for the final realization of your hope, so that you won't become lazy, but imitators of those who inherit the promises through faith and perseverance.

Hebrews 6:11-12

GOD'S PURPOSE

For I know the plans I have for you"—[this is]the
Lord's declaration—"plans for [your]welfare, not for
disaster, to give you a future and a hope.
Jeremiah 29:11

God never creates anything without a purpose in mind.
All things were created by an act of His will and that
includes you. God knew you before you were in your
mother's womb, and no matter how many bad choices
and decisions you have made, He desires to use you to
fulfill His mission on the earth. No matter how difficult
or confusing life may be, God can use you, right where
you are.

All your talent and ability as a singer and musician
came from God. You may not be the finest musician
in the world, but He has used musicians of all kinds
throughout the ages to accomplish His purpose on the
earth. It is not always the most talented who produce
the greatest results. The key is to develop the talent
and ability He has given through disciplined effort,
and to submit all that you have to His will and purpose
for your life.

Your life is filled with purpose on many levels. You
have purpose as a friend, a brother or sister, a son or

daughter, a father or mother. You have purpose as an employer or servant, a leader or follower. Whatever your station or role in life, God has a purpose for you.

As a singer and musician, you were created to inspire God's people as you proclaim His truth, His mercy and His goodness to those He puts in front of you. God's purpose for you is to lead His people into His presence. God created singers and musicians to precede His presence, His power, and His Word. Singers and musicians are called to lead His people as they celebrate, thank and praise the Lord.

As you study His Word, you will see how His great and precious promises apply to you in every walk of life. No matter what you have been told by the world or even those who love you, God has a special plan for your life.

God never makes anything without a clear purpose. And as you receive and believe and act upon His promises, you will discover and fulfill His unique purpose for your life.

———————————

Because by Him everything was created, in heaven and on earth, the visible and the invisible, whether thrones or dominions or rulers or authorities—all things have been created through Him and for Him.

Colossians 1:16

For we are His creation—created in Christ Jesus for
good works, which God prepared ahead of time so
that we should walk in them.

                                        Ephesians 2:10

Who has saved us and called us with a holy calling,
not according to our works, but according to His own
purpose and grace, which was given to us in Christ
Jesus before time began.

                                        2 Timothy 1:9

In Him we were also made His inheritance, predestined
according to the purpose of the One who works out
everything in agreement with the decision of His will,
so that we who had already put our hope in the Messiah
might bring praise to His glory.

                                        Ephesians 1:11-12

He appointed some of the Levites as ministers before
the ark of the LORD, even to celebrate and to thank
and praise the LORD God of Israel:

                                        1 Chronicles 16:4 (NAS)

Go, therefore, and make disciples of all nations,
baptizing them in the name of the Father and of the
Son and of the Holy Spirit, teaching them to observe

everything I have commanded you. And remember,
I am with you always,to the end of the age."

Matthew 28:19-20

However, I have let you live for this purpose: to show you
My power and to make My name known in all the earth.

Exodus 9:16

"I assure you: The one who believes in Me will also
do the works that I do. And he will do even greater
works than these, because I am going to the Father.

John 14:12

LIFE'S PROCESS

We know that all things work together for the good
of those who love God: those who are called
according to His purpose.
Romans 8:28

The real challenge for most Christians is to believe and act upon the promises of God in the midst of the process of life. It often takes great faith and perseverance to see God's promises fulfilled. But that has been true since the beginning of time.

The Bible is filled with stories of our faith heroes who navigated the same process of life. Abraham is a great example. The Father of Our Faith was fully human just like you and me. Abraham got into God's presence, received God's promises, understood his purpose, and struggled mightily through the process until he reached his potential and blessed "all the people of the earth."

Abraham withstood the failures and trials of his own life's process and released his God-given potential that still affects every believer even today. He didn't go through life without challenges, and he certainly failed to meet the mark along the way. But he did have faith that God would fulfill His promises, and so must we.

The promises of God must be received and believed by faith. Faith requires both belief and action because faith without works is dead. And throughout the process of life, all things that are received by faith will be tested. That's where patience, endurance, and perseverance must come into play.

Faith is a powerful force, but it must be applied in combination with the force of patience. Hearing God's Word leads to faith. But when faith is tested, it takes patience, endurance, and perseverance to stand strong and receive God's promises. God truly is a rewarder of those who believe that He is and who diligently seek Him. He is not hiding, but He is always allowing the process of life to perfect our faith. He wants us to be perfect and complete, lacking nothing.

As we encounter the process of life, we can always know how we are doing by our words, our thoughts, and our actions.

Think about the last time you faced a trial. Or perhaps you are in the midst of one right now. Stop for a moment and take a look at how you responded. If your response was fear, doubt, anger, or manipulation, this is a clear indication that you are off track.

**Our response to the challenges of life should
always include prayer, perseverance, patience,
and praise.**

When you find yourself missing the mark during the
process, take the time to get back into His presence.
Run to His presence and *pray. Persevere* by continuing
to press on despite the opposition. Let *patience* have
its perfect work in the midst of the process, so that
you may be perfect and complete, lacking nothing
(James 1:4). Remember that God wants you to grow
through the trial, not just be rescued from it.

And *praise* God in the midst of your circumstance.
God inhabits the praises of His people. So when you
praise the Lord, you are actually inviting Him into your
circumstance and where the King is present, all things
are possible!

His great and precious promises are all you need for
life and godliness, and they are essential. They will see
you through every challenge you will ever face as you
believe and act upon them.

Do not be conformed to this age, but be transformed
by the renewing of your mind, so that you may discern
what is the good, pleasing, and perfect will of God.

Romans 12:2

Brothers, I do not consider myself to have taken hold of it. But one thing I do: forgetting what is behind and reaching forward to what is ahead, I pursue as my goal the prize promised by God's heavenly call in Christ Jesus.

Philippians 3:13-14

So don't throw away your confidence, which has a great reward. For you need endurance, so that after you have done God's will, you may receive what was promised.

Hebrews 10:35-36

Therefore let us approach the throne of grace with boldness, so that we may receive mercy and find grace to help us at the proper time.

Hebrews 4:16

Consider it a great joy, my brothers, whenever you experience various trials, knowing that the testing of your faith produces endurance. But endurance must do its complete work, so that you may be mature and complete, lacking nothing.

James 1:2-4

The Lord watches over the blameless all their days, and their inheritance will last forever. They will not be disgraced in times of adversity; they will be satisfied in days of hunger. A man's steps are established by the Lord, and He takes pleasure in his way. Though he falls, he will not be overwhelmed, because the Lord holds his hand.

Psalm 37:18-19, 23-24

Therefore we do not give up; even though our outer person is being destroyed, our inner person is being renewed day by day. For our momentary light affliction is producing for us an absolutely incomparable eternal weight of glory. So we do not focus on what is seen, but on what is unseen; for what is seen is temporary, but what is unseen is eternal.

2 Corinthians 4:16-18

Finally, be strengthened by the Lord and by His vast strength. Put on the full armor of God so that you can stand against the tactics of the Devil. For our battle is not against flesh and blood, but against the rulers, against the authorities, against the world powers of this darkness, against the spiritual forces of evil in the heavens.

Ephesians 6:10-12

Finally brothers, whatever is true, whatever is honorable, whatever is just, whatever is pure, whatever is lovely, whatever is commendable—if there is any moral excellence and if there is any praise—dwell on these things.

Philippians 4:8

YOUR POTENTIAL

Now to Him who is able to do above and beyond
all that we ask or think—
according to the power that works in you.
Ephesians 3:20

We are the body of Christ, and God wants us to impact those around us. At the cross, Jesus declared it was finished and shortly thereafter took His rightful position at the right hand of the Father. Jesus is the head and we are His body on this earth. God has chosen to do His work through us.

That is the mystery that the Apostle Paul revealed to believers for all the ages—Christ is in you, willing and doing His good pleasure. We are the ones who will manifest His love and works in our generation. Because we are His and He has chosen to dwell in us and operate through us, there is great potential—great dormant and hidden power in us. God wants to release that power for His purposes and His glory.

We can see throughout Scripture that there will always be obstacles to God's work on this earth. The clash of the kingdom of this world and the kingdom of heaven is visible every day as we navigate the process of life.

That process is the fuel that ignites the Word within you and releases your potential.

As you step out in faith and use the gifts, talent, and ability that God has placed in you, you will encounter opposition. The battle for the minds, hearts, and souls of this generation is intense. But fear not, for God has given us mighty weapons of warfare to overcome every principality and power that we will ever encounter.

Every time you sing or play, you have the opportunity to set aside the struggles of this life and lead God's people into His presence. That is your purpose as a singer and musician, and that is where your potential is released. As you proclaim Jesus as Lord and glorify the King of kings, you are releasing the power of God to affect those who hear your expression of worship.

Jesus came to heal the sick, bind up the brokenhearted and set the captives free. His mission today is still the same. He chose you and gave you talent and ability to lead people into His presence. God created you to be a unique tool of proclamation. As you surrender to His will, He will flow through you and change lives.

Everything you need is already inside you.

For it is God who is working in you, [enabling you] both to will and to act for His good purpose.

Philippians 2:13

I am able to do all things through Him who strengthens me.

Philippians 4:13

" I assure you: The one who believes in Me will also do the works that I do. And he will do even greater works than these, because I am going to the Father."

John 14:12

But you will receive power when the Holy Spirit has come upon you, and you will be My witnesses in Jerusalem, in all Judea and Samaria, and to the ends of the earth."

Acts 1:8

So because of Christ, I am pleased in weaknesses, in insults, in catastrophes, in persecutions, and in pressures. For when I am weak, then I am strong.

2 Corinthians 12:10

And if the Spirit of Him who raised Jesus from the dead lives in you, then He who raised Christ from the dead will also bring your mortal bodies to life through His Spirit who lives in you.

Romans 8:11

And these signs will accompany those who believe:
In My name they will drive out demons; they will
speak in new languages; they will pick up snakes;
if they should drink anything deadly, it will never
harm them; they will lay hands on the sick, and they
will get well."

Mark 16:17-18

He said to them, "I watched Satan fall from heaven
like a lightning flash. Look, I have given you the
authority to trample on snakes and scorpions and
over all the power of the enemy; nothing will ever
harm you.

Luke 10:18-19

I have been crucified with Christ; and I no longer
live, but Christ lives in me. The life I now live in
the flesh, I live by faith in the Son of God, who
loved me and gave Himself for me.

Galatians 2:20

For me, living is Christ and dying is gain.

Philippians 1:21

Great and Precious Promises

When you are… AFRAID
For God has not given us a spirit of fearfulness, but one of power, love, and sound judgment.

2 Timothy 1:7

There is no fear in love; instead, perfect love drives out fear, because fear involves punishment. So the one who fears has not reached perfection in love.

1 John 4:18

For you did not receive a spirit of slavery to fall back into fear, but you received the Spirit of adoption, by whom we cry out, "*Abba*, Father!" The Spirit Himself testifies together with our spirit that we are God's children.

Romans 8:15-16

The one who lives under the protection of the Most High dwells in the shadow of the Almighty. I will say to the Lord, "My refuge and my fortress, my God, in whom I trust."

Psalm 91:1-2

Do not fear, for I am with you; do not be afraid, for I am your God. I will strengthen you; I will help you; I will hold on to you with My righteous right hand.

Isaiah 41:10

Don't fear sudden danger or the ruin of the wicked when it comes, for the Lord will be your confidence and will keep your foot from a snare.

Proverbs 3:25-26

And you will be established on [a foundation of] righteousness. You will be far from oppression, you will certainly not be afraid; you will be far from terror, it will certainly not come near you.

Isaiah 54:14

Even when I go through the darkest valley, I fear [no] danger, for You are with me; Your rod and Your staff—they comfort me. You prepare a table before me in the presence of my enemies; You anoint my head with oil; my cup overflows.

Psalm 23:4-5

The Lord is my light and my salvation—whom should I fear? The Lord is the stronghold of my life— of whom should I be afraid?

Psalm 27:1

Peace I leave with you, My peace I give to you; not as the world gives do I give to you. Let not your heart be troubled, neither let it be afraid.

John 14:27

When you are...ANGRY

My dearly loved brothers, understand this: everyone must be quick to hear, slow to speak, and slow to anger, for man's anger does not accomplish God's righteousness.

James 1:19-20

Be angry and do not sin. Don't let the sun go down on your anger.

Ephesians 4:26

A gentle answer turns away anger, but a harsh word stirs up wrath.

Proverbs 15:1

A patient person [shows] great understanding,
but a quick-tempered one promotes foolishness.

Proverbs 14:29

Don't let your spirit rush to be angry, for anger abides
in the heart of fools.

Ecclesiastes 7:9

All bitterness, anger and wrath, insult and slander
must be removed from you, along with all wickedness.
And be kind and compassionate to one another,
forgiving one another, just as God also forgave you
in Christ.

Ephesians 4:31-32

So if you are offering your gift on the altar, and
there you remember that your brother has something
against you, leave your gift there in front of the altar.
First go and be reconciled with your brother, and then
come and offer your gift.

Matthew 5:23-24

But now you must also put away all the following:
anger, wrath, malice, slander, and filthy language
from your mouth.

Colossians 3:8

Refrain from anger and give up [your] rage; do not be agitated—it can only bring harm.

Psalm 37:8

For our battle is not against flesh and blood, but against the rulers, against the authorities, against the world powers of this darkness, against the spiritual forces of evil in the heavens.

Ephesians 6:12

When you are…CONFUSED
Don't worry about anything, but in everything, through prayer and petition with thanksgiving, let your requests be made known to God. And the peace of God, which surpasses every thought, will guard your hearts and your minds in Christ Jesus.

Philippians 4:6-7

For: who has known the Lord's mind, that he may instruct Him? But we have the mind of Christ.

1 Corinthians 2:16

In the same way the Spirit also joins to help in our weakness, because we do not know what to pray for as we should, but the Spirit Himself intercedes for us with unspoken groanings. And He who searches the hearts knows the Spirit's mind-set, because He intercedes for the saints according to the will of God.

Romans 8:26-27

For God is not the author of confusion but of peace, as in all the churches of the saints.

1 Corinthians 14:33(NKJV)

Your word is a lamp for my feet and a light on my path.

Psalm 119:105

For where envy and selfish ambition exist, there is disorder and every kind of evil. But the wisdom from above is first pure, then peace-loving, gentle, compliant, full of mercy and good fruits, without favoritism and hypocrisy.

James 3:16-17

Now if any of you lacks wisdom, he should ask God, who gives to all generously and without criticizing, and it will be given to him.

James 1:5

Trust in the Lord with all your heart, and do not rely on your own understanding; think about Him in all your ways, and He will guide you on the right paths.

Proverbs 3:5-6

I will instruct you and teach you in the way you should go; I will guide you with My eye.

Psalm 32:8 (NKJV)

Your eyes will see your Teacher, and whenever you turn to the right or to the left, your ears will hear this command behind you: "This is the way. Walk in it."

Isaiah 30:21

When you are…DEPRESSED
The righteous cry out, and the Lord hears, and delivers them from all their troubles.

Psalm 34:17

I will be with you when you pass through the waters, and [when you pass] through the rivers, they will not overwhelm you. You will not be scorched when you walk through the fire, and the flame will not burn you.

Isaiah 43:2

For His anger lasts only a moment, but His favor, a lifetime. Weeping may spend the night, but there is joy in the morning.

Psalm 30:5

But those who wait on the LORD shall renew their strength; they shall mount up with wings like eagles, they shall run and not be weary, they shall walk and not faint.

Isaiah 40:31 (NKJV)

Blessed be the God and Father of our Lord Jesus Christ, the Father of mercies and the God of all comfort. He comforts us in all our affliction, so that we may be able to comfort those who are in any kind of affliction, through the comfort we ourselves receive from God.

2 Corinthians 1:3-4

For I am persuaded that neither death nor life, nor angels nor rulers, nor things present, nor things to come, nor powers, nor height, nor depth, nor any other created thing will have the power to separate us from the love of God that is in Christ Jesus our Lord!

Romans 8:38-39

Finally brothers, whatever is true, whatever is honorable, whatever is just, whatever is pure, whatever is lovely, whatever is commendable—if there is any moral excellence and if there is any praise—dwell on these things.

Philippians 4:8

Humble yourselves therefore under the mighty hand of God, so that He may exalt you in due time, casting all your care upon Him, because He cares about you.

1 Peter 5:6-7

Do not grieve, because your strength [comes from] rejoicing in the Lord."

Nehemiah 8:10b

Yet He Himself bore our sicknesses, and He carried our pains; but we in turn regarded Him stricken, struck down by God, and afflicted. But He was pierced because of our transgressions, crushed because of our iniquities; punishment for our peace was on Him, and we are healed by His wounds.

Isaiah 53:4-5

When you are...DISCOURAGED

"Blessed are the poor in spirit, because the kingdom of heaven is theirs. Blessed are those who mourn, because they will be comforted. Blessed are the gentle, because they will inherit the earth. Blessed are those who hunger and thirst for righteousness, because they will be filled. Blessed are the merciful, because they will be shown mercy. Blessed are the pure in heart, because they will see God. Blessed are the peacemakers, because they will be called sons of God. Blessed are those who are persecuted for righteousness, because the kingdom of heaven is theirs.

Matthew 5:3-10

So we must not get tired of doing good, for we will reap at the proper time if we don't give up.

Galatians 6:9

Be of good courage, and He shall strengthen your heart, all you who hope in the Lord.

Psalm 31:24 (NKJV)

Now the God of all grace, who called you to His eternal glory in Christ Jesus, will personally restore, establish, strengthen, and support you after you have suffered a little.

1 Peter 5:10

No weapon formed against you will succeed, and you will refute any accusation raised against you in court. This is the heritage of the Lord's servants, and their righteousness is from Me."

Isaiah 54:17

If I walk in the thick of danger, You will preserve my life from the anger of my enemies. You will extend Your hand; Your right hand will save me.

Psalm 138:7

"Peace I leave with you. My peace I give to you. I do not give to you as the world gives. Your heart must not be troubled or fearful.

John 14:27

We are pressured in every way but not crushed; we are perplexed but not in despair; we are persecuted but not abandoned; we are struck down but not destroyed.

2 Corinthians 4:8-9

So don't throw away your confidence, which has a great reward. For you need endurance, so that after you have done God's will, you may receive what was promised.

Hebrews 10:35-36

When you are...HAVING DOUBTS

Trust in the Lord with all your heart, and do not rely on your own understanding; think about Him in all your ways, and He will guide you on the right paths.

Proverbs 3:5-6

Do not fear, for I am with you; do not be afraid, for I am your God. I will strengthen you; I will help you; I will hold on to you with My righteous right hand.

Isaiah 41:10

Cast your burden on the Lord, and He will support you; He will never allow the righteous to be shaken.

Psalm 55:22

Don't worry about anything, but in everything, through prayer and petition with thanksgiving, let your requests be made known to God. And the peace of God, which surpasses every thought, will guard your hearts and your minds in Christ Jesus.

Philippians 4:6-7

For I am persuaded that neither death nor life, nor angels nor rulers, nor things present, nor things to come, nor powers, nor height, nor depth, nor any other created thing will have the power to separate us from the love of God that is in Christ Jesus our Lord!

Romans 8:38-39

When you are…MISTREATED/DECEIVED

Pursue peace with everyone, and holiness—without it no one will see the Lord. See to it that no one falls short of the grace of God and that no root of bitterness springs up, causing trouble and by it, defiling many.

Hebrews 12:14-15

Do not be deceived: "Bad company corrupts good morals." Become right-minded and stop sinning, because some people are ignorant about God. I say this to your shame.

1 Corinthians 15:33-34

In fact, all those who want to live a godly life in Christ Jesus will be persecuted. Evil people and imposters will become worse, deceiving and being deceived. But as for you, continue in what you have learned and firmly believed, knowing those from whom you learned.

2 Timothy 3:12-14

When you are...REJECTED

Therefore, God's chosen ones, holy and loved, put on heartfelt compassion, kindness, humility, gentleness, and patience, accepting one another and forgiving one another if anyone has a complaint against another. Just as the Lord has forgiven you, so also you must [forgive]. Above all, [put on] love—the perfect bond of unity.

Colossians 3:12-14

But I tell you, love your enemies and pray for those who persecute you.

Matthew 5:44

All bitterness, anger and wrath, insult and slander must be removed from you, along with all wickedness. And be kind and compassionate to one another, forgiving one another, just as God also forgave you in Christ.

Ephesians 4:31-32

Man does not see what the Lord sees, for man sees what is visible, but the Lord sees the heart."

1 Samuel 16:7b

No, in all these things we are more than victorious through Him who loved us.

Romans 8:37

But if [anyone suffers] as a Christian, he should not
be ashamed, but should glorify God with that name.

1 Peter 4:16

The Lord is near the brokenhearted; He saves those
crushed in spirit.

Psalm 34:18

Blessed are those who are persecuted for righteousness,
because the kingdom of heaven is theirs. "Blessed
are you when they insult you and persecute you and
falsely say every kind of evil against you because of
Me. Be glad and rejoice, because your reward is great
in heaven. For that is how they persecuted the prophets
who were before you.

Matthew 5:10-12

Commit your way to the Lord; trust in Him, and He
will act, making your righteousness shine like the
dawn, your justice like the noonday. Be silent before
the Lord and wait expectantly for Him; do not be
agitated by one who prospers in his way, by the man
who carries out evil plans.

Psalm 37:5-7

When you are…TEMPTED
No temptation has overtaken you except what is common to humanity. God is faithful and He will not allow you to be tempted beyond what you are able, but with the temptation He will also provide a way of escape, so that you are able to bear it.

1 Corinthians 10:13

Finally, brethren, whatever things are true, whatever things are noble, whatever things are just, whatever things are pure, whatever things are lovely, whatever things are of good report, if there is any virtue and if there is anything praiseworthy—meditate on these things.

Philippians 4:8 (NKJV)

"Stay awake and pray, so that you won't enter into temptation. The spirit is willing, but the flesh is weak."

Matthew 26:41

Blessed is a man who endures trials, because when he passes the test he will receive the crown of life that He has promised to those who love Him. No one undergoing a trial should say, "I am being tempted by God." For God is not tempted by evil, and He Himself doesn't tempt anyone.

James 1:12-13

For since He Himself was tested and has suffered, He is able to help those who are tested.

Hebrews 2:18

For we do not have a high priest who is unable to sympathize with our weaknesses, but One who has been tested in every way as we are, yet without sin.

Hebrews 4:15

Therefore, submit to God. But resist the Devil, and he will flee from you. Draw near to God, and He will draw near to you.

James 4:7-8

Dear friends, when the fiery ordeal arises among you to test you, don't be surprised by it, as if something unusual were happening to you. Instead, as you share in the sufferings of the Messiah rejoice, so that you may also rejoice with great joy at the revelation of His glory.

1 Peter 4:12-13

When you are...UNDISCIPLINED

You must submit to and endure [correction] for
discipline; God is dealing with you as with sons. For
what son is there whom his father does not [thus]
train and correct and discipline? Now if you are
exempt from correction and left without discipline
in which all [of God's children] share, then you are
illegitimate offspring and not true sons [at all].

Hebrews 12:7-8 (AMP)

For the time being no discipline brings joy, but
seems grievous and painful; but afterwards it yields
a peaceable fruit of righteousness to those who have
been trained by it [a harvest of fruit which consists
in righteousness—in conformity to God's will in
purpose, thought, and action, resulting in right living
and right standing with God].

Hebrews 12:11 (AMP)

Instead, I discipline my body and bring it under strict
control, so that after preaching to others, I myself will
not be disqualified.

1 Corinthians 9:27

The reverent and worshipful fear of the Lord is
the beginning and the principal and choice part of
knowledge [its starting point and its essence]; but

fools despise skillful and godly Wisdom, instruction, and discipline.

Proverbs 1:7 (AMP)

Therefore I always exercise and discipline myself [mortifying my body, deadening my carnal affections, bodily appetites, and worldly desires, endeavoring in all respects] to have a clear (unshaken, blameless) conscience, void of offense toward God and toward men.

Acts 24:16 (AMP)

For God did not give us a spirit of timidity (of cowardice, of craven and cringing and fawning fear), but [He has given us a spirit] of power and of love and of calm and well-balanced mind and discipline and self-control.

2 Timothy 1:7 (AMP)

When you are...WAITING

Now we want each of you to demonstrate the same diligence for the final realization of your hope, so that you won't become lazy, but imitators of those who inherit the promises through faith and perseverance.

Hebrews 6:11-12

Like a servant's eyes on His master's hand, like a servant girl's eyes on her mistress's hand, so our eyes are on the Lord our God until He shows us favor.

Psalm 123:2

From ancient times no one has heard, no one has listened, no eye has seen any God except You, who acts on behalf of the one who waits for Him.

Isaiah 64:4

Guide me in Your truth and teach me, for You are the God of my salvation; I wait for You all day long.

Psalm 25:5

I waited patiently for the Lord, and He turned to me and heard my cry for help. He brought me up from a desolate pit, out of the muddy clay, and set my feet on a rock, making my steps secure.

Psalm 40:1-2

Wait for the Lord; be courageous and let your heart be strong. Wait for the Lord.

Psalm 27:14

But those who wait on the LORD shall renew their strength; they shall mount up with wings like eagles, they shall run and not be weary, they shall walk and not faint.

Isaiah 40:31 (NKJV)

The end of a matter is better than its beginning; a patient spirit is better than a proud spirit.

Ecclesiastes 7:8

Therefore, brothers, be patient until the Lord's coming. See how the farmer waits for the precious fruit of the earth and is patient with it until it receives the early and the late rains. You also must be patient. Strengthen your hearts, because the Lord's coming is near.

James 5:7-8

When you are...WORRIED

Don't worry about anything, but in everything, through prayer and petition with thanksgiving, let your requests be made known to God. And the peace of God, which surpasses every thought, will guard your hearts and your minds in Christ Jesus.

Philippians 4:6-7

"Your heart must not be troubled. Believe in God; believe also in Me.

John 14:1

"Peace I leave with you. My peace I give to you. I do not give to you as the world gives. Your heart must not be troubled or fearful.

John 14:27

And my God will supply all your needs according to His riches in glory in Christ Jesus.

Philippians 4:19

I will both lie down and sleep in peace, for You alone, Lord, make me live in safety.

Psalm 4:8

"This is why I tell you: Don't worry about your life, what you will eat or what you will drink; or about your body, what you will wear. Isn't life more than food and the body more than clothing? Look at the birds of the sky: they don't sow or reap or gather into barns, yet your heavenly Father feeds them. Aren't you worth more than they?

Matthew 6:25-26

For the mind-set of the flesh is death, but the mind-set of the Spirit is life and peace.

Romans 8:6

You will keep in perfect peace the mind [that is] dependent [on You], for it is trusting in You.

Isaiah 26:3

When you lie down, you will not be afraid; you will lie down, and your sleep will be pleasant.

Proverbs 3:24

Abundant peace belongs to those who love Your instruction; nothing makes them stumble.

Psalm 119:165

The one who lives under the protection of the Most High dwells in the shadow of the Almighty. I will say to the Lord, "My refuge and my fortress, my God, in whom I trust." He Himself will deliver you from the hunter's net, from the destructive plague. He will cover you with His feathers; you will take refuge under His wings. His faithfulness will be a protective shield.

Psalm 91:1-4

What the Bible says about...FAITH
Now faith is the substance of things hoped for, the
evidence of things not seen.

Hebrews 11:1 (NKJV)

So then faith comes by hearing, and hearing by the
word of God.

Romans 10:17 (NKJV)

So we do not focus on what is seen, but on what is
unseen; for what is seen is temporary, but what is
unseen is eternal.

2 Corinthians 4:18

For by grace you are saved through faith, and this
is not from yourselves; it is God's gift—not from
works, so that no one can boast.

Ephesians 2:8-9

Now without faith it is impossible to please God, for
the one who draws near to Him must believe that He
exists and rewards those who seek Him.

Hebrews 11:6

Now we want each of you to demonstrate the same diligence for the final realization of your hope, so that you won't become lazy, but imitators of those who inherit the promises through faith and perseverance.

Hebrews 6:11-12

In the same way faith, if it doesn't have works, is dead by itself.

James 2:17

But My righteous one will live by faith; and if he draws back, My soul has no pleasure in him.

Hebrews 10:38

Whatever has been born of God conquers the world. This is the victory that has conquered the world: our faith.

1 John 5:4

"Because of your little faith," He told them. "For I assure you: If you have faith the size of a mustard seed, you will tell this mountain, 'Move from here to there,' and it will move. Nothing will be impossible for you.

Matthew 17:20

For we walk by faith, not by sight.

                                          2 Corinthians 5:7

Therefore, since we have been declared righteous
by faith, we have peace with God through our Lord
Jesus Christ. Also through Him, we have obtained
access by faith into this grace in which we stand, and
we rejoice in the hope of the glory of God.

                                          Romans 5:1-2

What the Bible says about…FEAR
The Lord is for me; I will not be afraid. What can
man do to me?

                                          Psalm 118:6

For God has not given us a spirit of fearfulness, but
one of power, love, and sound judgment.

                                          2 Timothy 1:7

There is no fear in love; instead, perfect love drives
out fear, because fear involves punishment. So the
one who fears has not reached perfection in love.

                                          1 John 4:18

For you did not receive a spirit of slavery to fall back
into fear, but you received the Spirit of adoption, by

whom we cry out, "*Abba*, Father!"

Romans 8:15

Yea, though I walk through the valley of the shadow of death, I will fear no evil; for You are with me; Your rod and Your staff, they comfort me.

Psalm 23:4 (NKJV)

But whoever listens to me will live securely and be free from the fear of danger."

Proverbs 1:33

Happy is the man who fears the Lord, taking great delight in His commandments.

Psalm 112:1

Do not fear, for I am with you; do not be afraid, for I am your God. I will strengthen you; I will help you; I will hold on to you with My righteous right hand.

Isaiah 41:10

Aren't five sparrows sold for two pennies? Yet not one of them is forgotten in God's sight. Indeed, the hairs of your head are all counted. Don't be afraid; you are worth more than many sparrows!

Luke 12:6-7

Now since the children have flesh and blood in common, He also shared in these, so that through His death He might destroy the one holding the power of death—that is, the Devil— and free those who were held in slavery all their lives by the fear of death.

Hebrews 2:14-15

What the Bible says about...FINANCES
"Bring the full 10 percent into the storehouse so that there may be food in My house. Test Me in this way," says the Lord of Hosts. "See if I will not open the floodgates of heaven and pour out a blessing for you without measure. I will rebuke the devourer for you, so that it will not ruin the produce of your ground, and your vine in your field will not be barren," says the Lord of Hosts.

Malachi 3:10-11

Remember this: the person who sows sparingly will also reap sparingly, and the person who sows generously will also reap generously. Each person should do as he has decided in his heart—not out of regret or out of necessity, for God loves a cheerful giver. And God is able to make every grace overflow to you, so that in every way, always having everything you need, you may excel in every good work.

2 Corinthians 9: 6-8

Give, and it will be given to you; a good measure—
pressed down, shaken together, and running over—
will be poured into your lap. For with the measure
you use, it will be measured back to you."

Luke 6:38

Not that I seek or am eager for [your] gift, but I
do seek and am eager for the fruit which increases
to your credit [the harvest of blessing that is
accumulating to your account].

Philippians 4:17 (AMP)

Sitting across from the temple treasury, He watched
how the crowd dropped money into the treasury.
Many rich people were putting in large sums. And
a poor widow came and dropped in two tiny coins
worth very little. Summoning His disciples, He said
to them, "I assure you: This poor widow has put in
more than all those giving to the temple treasury.
For they all gave out of their surplus, but she out of
her poverty has put in everything she possessed—all
she had to live on."

Mark 12:41-44

But those who want to be rich fall into temptation, a trap, and many foolish and harmful desires, which plunge people into ruin and destruction. For the love of money is a root of all kinds of evil, and by craving it, some have wandered away from the faith and pierced themselves with many pains. Now you, man of God, run from these things; but pursue righteousness, godliness, faith, love, endurance, and gentleness.

1 Timothy 6:9-11

What the Bible says about...FORGIVENESS
In Him we have redemption through His blood, the forgiveness of our trespasses, according to the riches of His grace that He lavished on us with all wisdom and understanding.

Ephesians 1:7-8

If we say, "We have no sin," we are deceiving ourselves, and the truth is not in us. If we confess our sins, He is faithful and righteous to forgive us our sins and to cleanse us from all unrighteousness. If we say, "We have not sinned," we make Him a liar, and His word is not in us.

1 John 1:8-10

As far as the east is from the west, so far has He removed our transgressions from us.

Psalm 103:12

For if you forgive people their wrongdoing, your heavenly Father will forgive you as well. But if you don't forgive people, your Father will not forgive your wrongdoing.

Matthew 6:14-15

Do not judge, and you will not be judged. Do not condemn, and you will not be condemned. Forgive, and you will be forgiven.

Luke 6:37

Be on your guard. If your brother sins, rebuke him, and if he repents, forgive him. And if he sins against you seven times in a day, and comes back to you seven times, saying, "I repent," you must forgive him.

Luke 17:3-4

And whenever you stand praying, if you have anything against anyone, forgive him, so that your Father in heaven will also forgive you your wrongdoing.

Mark 11:25

But I tell you, love your enemies and pray for those who persecute you, so that you may be sons of your Father in heaven.

Matthew 5:44

All bitterness, anger and wrath, insult and slander must be removed from you, along with all wickedness. And be kind and compassionate to one another, forgiving one another, just as God also forgave you in Christ.

Ephesians 4:31-32

What the Bible says about...HEALING
Yet He Himself bore our sicknesses, and He carried our pains; but we in turn regarded Him stricken, struck down by God, and afflicted. But He was pierced because of our transgressions, crushed because of our iniquities; punishment for our peace was on Him, and we are healed by His wounds.

Isaiah 53:4-5

He Himself bore our sins in His body on the tree, so that, having died to sins, we might live for righteousness; by His wounding you have been healed.

1 Peter 2:24

My soul, praise the Lord, and all that is within me,
praise His holy name. My soul, praise the Lord, and
do not forget all His benefits. He forgives all your
sin; He heals all your diseases.

Psalm 103:1-3

Is anyone among you sick? He should call for the elders of
the church, and they should pray over him after anointing
him with olive oil in the name of the Lord. The prayer of
faith will save the sick person, and the Lord will raise him
up; and if he has committed sins, he will be forgiven.

James 5:14-15

And these signs will accompany those who believe: In
My name they will drive out demons; they will speak
in new languages; they will pick up snakes; if they
should drink anything deadly, it will never harm them;
they will lay hands on the sick, and they will get well."

Mark 16:17-18

My son, pay attention to my words; listen closely
to my sayings. Don't lose sight of them; keep them
within your heart. For they are life to those who find
them, and health to one's whole body.

Proverbs 4:20-22

If you diligently heed the voice of the Lord your God
and do what is right in His sight, give ear to His
commandments and keep all His statutes, I will put
none of the diseases on you which I have brought on
the Egyptians. For I am the Lord who heals you.

Exodus 15:26 (NKJV)

Worship the Lord your God, and He will bless your
bread and your water. I will take away your illnesses.

Exodus 23:25

Then they cried out to the Lord in their trouble; He
saved them from their distress. He sent His word and
healed them; He rescued them from the Pit.

Psalm 107:19-20

Dear friend, I pray that you may prosper in every way
and be in good health, just as your soul prospers.

3 John 1:2

What the Bible says about…HOPE
For whatever was written before was written for
our instruction, so that through our endurance and
through the encouragement of the Scriptures we may
have hope.

Romans 15:4

Let us hold on to the confession of our hope without wavering, for He who promised is faithful.

Hebrews 10:23

Now may the God of hope fill you with all joy and peace in believing, so that you may overflow with hope by the power of the Holy Spirit.

Romans 15:13

Blessed be the God and Father of our Lord Jesus Christ. According to His great mercy, He has given us a new birth into a living hope through the resurrection of Jesus Christ from the dead, and into an inheritance that is imperishable, uncorrupted, and unfading, kept in heaven for you.

1 Peter 1:3-4

Now in this hope we were saved, yet hope that is seen is not hope, because who hopes for what he sees? But if we hope for what we do not see, we eagerly wait for it with patience.

Romans 8:24-25

And not only that, but we also rejoice in our afflictions, because we know that affliction produces endurance, endurance produces proven character, and proven character produces hope. This hope does not disappoint,

because God's love has been poured out in our hearts
through the Holy Spirit who was given to us.

Romans 5:3-5

We have this [hope]—like a sure and firm anchor
of the soul—that enters the inner sanctuary behind
the curtain. Jesus has entered there on our behalf as
a forerunner, because He has become a "high priest
forever in the order of Melchizedek."

Hebrews 6:19-20

But set apart the Messiah as Lord in your hearts, and
always be ready to give a defense to anyone who asks
you for a reason for the hope that is in you.

1 Peter 3:15

What the Bible says about…LOVE
Love the Lord your God with all your heart, with
all your soul, with all your mind, and with all your
strength. "The second is: Love your neighbor as
yourself. There is no other commandment greater
than these."

Mark 12:30-31

This is My command: love one another as I have
loved you. No one has greater love than this, that

someone would lay down his life for his friends.
You are My friends if you do what I command you.

John 15:12-14

For God loved the world in this way: He gave His
One and Only Son, so that everyone who believes in
Him will not perish but have eternal life.

John 3:16

But God proves His own love for us in that while we
were still sinners Christ died for us!

Romans 5:8

Love consists in this: not that we loved God, but that
He loved us and sent His Son to be the propitiation
for our sins.

1 John 4:10

Dear friends, let us love one another, because love
is from God, and everyone who loves has been born
of God and knows God. The one who does not love
does not know God, because God is love.

1 John 4:7-8

This is how we have come to know love: He laid down
His life for us. We should also lay down our lives for

our brothers. If anyone has this world's goods and sees his brother in need but shuts off his compassion from him—how can God's love reside in him?

1 John 3:16-17

Above all, [put on] love—the perfect bond of unity.

Colossians 3:14

Love is patient; love is kind. Love does not envy; is not boastful; is not conceited; does not act improperly; is not selfish; is not provoked; does not keep a record of wrongs; finds no joy in unrighteousness, but rejoices in the truth; bears all things, believes all things, hopes all things, endures all things. Love never ends...Now these three remain: faith, hope, and love.

1 Corinthians 13:4-8, 13

What the Bible says about...REPENTANCE
If My people who are called by My name will humble themselves, and pray and seek My face, and turn from their wicked ways, then I will hear from heaven, and will forgive their sin and heal their land.

2 Chronicles 7:14 (NKJV)

If we confess our sins, He is faithful and righteous to
forgive us our sins and to cleanse us from all
unrighteousness.

1 John 1:9

Therefore repent and turn back, that your sins may
be wiped out so that seasons of refreshing may come
from the presence of the Lord.

Acts 3:19

"Therefore, having overlooked the times of ignorance,
God now commands all people everywhere to repent,
because He has set a day on which He is going to
judge the world in righteousness by the Man He has
appointed. He has provided proof of this to everyone
by raising Him from the dead."

Acts 17:30-31

He also said to them, "This is what is written: the
Messiah would suffer and rise from the dead the third
day, and repentance for forgiveness of sins would be
proclaimed in His name to all the nations, beginning
at Jerusalem.

Luke 24:46-47

Therefore if anyone is in Christ, there is a new creation; old things have passed away, and look, new things have come.

2 Corinthians 5:17

For God did not send His Son into the world that He might judge the world, but that the world might be saved through Him. Anyone who believes in Him is not judged, but anyone who does not believe is already judged, because he has not believed in the name of the One and Only Son of God.

John 3:17-18

When they heard this they became silent. Then they glorified God, saying, "So God has granted repentance resulting in life to even the Gentiles!"

Acts 11:18

Then I acknowledged my sin to You and did not conceal my iniquity. I said, "I will confess my transgressions to the Lord," and You took away the guilt of my sin. *Selah*

Psalm 32:5

What the Bible says about...SALVATION

"For God loved the world in this way: He gave His One and Only Son, so that everyone who believes in Him will not perish but have eternal life. For God did not send His Son into the world that He might judge the world, but that the world might be saved through Him. Anyone who believes in Him is not judged, but anyone who does not believe is already judged, because he has not believed in the name of the One and Only Son of God.

John 3:16-18

Jesus replied, "I assure you: Unless someone is born again, he cannot see the kingdom of God."

John 3:3

For the wages of sin is death, but the gift of God is eternal life in Christ Jesus our Lord.

Romans 6:23

But God proves His own love for us in that while we were still sinners Christ died for us!

Romans 5:8

For by grace you are saved through faith, and this is not from yourselves; it is God's gift—not from works, so that no one can boast.

Ephesians 2:8-9

...if you confess with your mouth, "Jesus is Lord," and believe in your heart that God raised Him from the dead, you will be saved.

Romans 10:9

And it shall come to pass that whoever calls on the name of the LORD shall be saved.

Acts 2:21 (NKJV)

For the grace of God has appeared, with salvation for all people, instructing us to deny godlessness and worldly lusts and to live in a sensible, righteous, and godly way in the present age.

Titus 2:11-12

He saved us—not by works of righteousness that we had done, but according to His mercy, through the washing of regeneration and renewal by the Holy Spirit.

Titus 3:5

So then, my dear friends, just as you have always obeyed, not only in my presence, but now even more in my absence, work out your own salvation with fear and trembling.

Philippians 2:12

What the Bible says about…SPIRITUAL WARFARE

Finally, be strengthened by the Lord and by His vast strength. Put on the full armor of God so that you can stand against the tactics of the Devil. For our battle is not against flesh and blood, but against the rulers, against the authorities, against the world powers of this darkness, against the spiritual forces of evil in the heavens. This is why you must take up the full armor of God, so that you may be able to resist in the evil day, and having prepared everything, to take your stand.

Ephesians 6:10-13

For although we are walking in the flesh, we do not wage war in a fleshly way, since the weapons of our warfare are not fleshly, but are powerful through God for the demolition of strongholds. We demolish arguments and every high-minded thing that is raised up against the knowledge of God, taking every thought captive to the obedience of Christ.

2 Corinthians 10:3-5

Therefore, submit to God. But resist the Devil, and he will flee from you. Draw near to God, and He will draw near to you.

James 4:7-8

Be sober! Be on the alert! Your adversary the Devil
is prowling around like a roaring lion, looking for
anyone he can devour. Resist him, firm in the faith,
knowing that the same sufferings are being experienced
by your brothers in the world.

1 Peter 5: 8-9

In the same way the Spirit also joins to help in our
weakness, because we do not know what to pray for
as we should, but the Spirit Himself intercedes for us
with unspoken groanings. And He who searches the
hearts knows the Spirit's mind-set, because He intercedes
for the saints according to the will of God.

Romans 8:26-27

Because whatever has been born of God conquers
the world. This is the victory that has conquered the
world: our faith.

1 John 5:4

But you, dear friends, building yourselves up in your
most holy faith and praying in the Holy Spirit, keep
yourselves in the love of God, expecting the mercy of
our Lord Jesus Christ for eternal life.

Jude 1:20-21

Dear friends, when the fiery ordeal arises among you to test you, don't be surprised by it, as if something unusual were happening to you. Instead, as you share in the sufferings of the Messiah rejoice, so that you may also rejoice with great joy at the revelation of His glory.

1 Peter 4:12-13

What the Bible says about…THE NAME OF JESUS
But these are written so that you may believe Jesus is the Messiah, the Son of God, and by believing you may have life in His name.

John 20:31

There is salvation in no one else, for there is no other name under heaven given to people by which we must be saved."

Acts 4:12

Then whoever calls on the name of the Lord will be saved.

Acts 2:21

For this reason God also highly exalted Him and gave Him the name that is above every name, so that at the name of Jesus every knee should bow—of those who are in heaven and on earth and under the earth—

and every tongue should confess that Jesus Christ is
Lord, to the glory of God the Father.

Philippians 2:9-11

Let the message about the Messiah dwell richly among
you, teaching and admonishing one another in all
wisdom, and singing psalms, hymns, and spiritual songs,
with gratitude in your hearts to God. And whatever you
do, in word or in deed, do everything in the name
of the Lord Jesus, giving thanks to God the Father
through Him.

Colossians 3:16-17

By faith in His name, His name has made this man
strong, whom you see and know. So the faith that
comes through Him has given him this perfect health
in front of all of you.

Acts 3:16

"I assure you: The one who believes in Me will also
do the works that I do. And he will do even greater
works than these, because I am going to the Father.
Whatever you ask in My name, I will do it so that
the Father may be glorified in the Son. If you ask Me
anything in My name, I will do it.

John 14:12-14

Then Jesus came near and said to them, "All authority has been given to Me in heaven and on earth. Go, therefore, and make disciples of all nations, baptizing them in the name of the Father and of the Son and of the Holy Spirit, teaching them to observe everything I have commanded you. And remember, I am with you always, to the end of the age."

Matthew 28:18-20

What the Bible says about...THE POWER OF THE BLOOD

According to the law almost everything is purified with blood, and without the shedding of blood there is no forgiveness.

Hebrews 9:22

Now the Messiah has appeared, high priest of the good things that have come. In the greater and more perfect tabernacle not made with hands (that is, not of this creation), He entered the holy of holies once for all, not by the blood of goats and calves, but by His own blood, having obtained eternal redemption. For if the blood of goats and bulls and the ashes of a heifer sprinkling those who are defiled, sanctify for the purification of the flesh, how much more will the blood of the Messiah, who through the eternal Spirit

offered Himself without blemish to God, cleanse our
consciences from dead works to serve the living God?

Hebrews 9:11-14

Then He took a cup, and after giving thanks, He gave
it to them and said, "Drink from it, all of you. For this
is My blood [that establishes] the covenant; it is shed
for many for the forgiveness of sins.

Matthew 26:27-28

Therefore, brothers, since we have boldness to enter
the sanctuary through the blood of Jesus, by the
new and living way that He has inaugurated for us,
through the curtain (that is, His flesh); and since we
have a great high priest over the house of God, let us
draw near with a true heart in full assurance of faith,
our hearts sprinkled [clean] from an evil conscience
and our bodies washed in pure water. Let us hold on
to the confession of our hope without wavering, for
He who promised is faithful.

Hebrews 10:19-23

For you know that you were redeemed from your
empty way of life inherited from the fathers, not with
perishable things, like silver or gold, but with the

precious blood of Christ, like that of a lamb without defect or blemish.

1 Peter 1:18-19

In Him we have redemption through His blood, the forgiveness of our trespasses, according to the riches of His grace.

Ephesians 1:7

At that time you were without the Messiah, excluded from the citizenship of Israel, and foreigners to the covenants of the promise, with no hope and without God in the world.

Ephesians 2:12

What the Bible says about…THE WORDS SPEAK
No rotten talk should come from your mouth, but only what is good for the building up of someone in need, in order to give grace to those who hear.

Ephesians 4:29

May the words of my mouth and the meditation of my heart be acceptable to You, Lord, my rock and my Redeemer.

Psalm 19:14

Life and death are in the power of the tongue, and
those who love it will eat its fruit.

Proverbs 18:21

I tell you that on the day of judgment people will
have to account for every careless word they speak.
For by your words you will be acquitted, and by your
words you will be condemned.

Matthew 12:36-37

And don't get drunk with wine, which [leads to] reckless
actions, but be filled with the Spirit: speaking to one
another in psalms, hymns, and spiritual songs, singing
and making music to the Lord in your heart, giving
thanks always for everything to God the Father in the
name of our Lord Jesus Christ,

Ephesians 5:18-20

They conquered him by the blood of the Lamb and by
the word of their testimony, for they did not love their
lives in the face of death.

Revelation 12:11

A good man produces good out of the good storeroom
of his heart. An evil man produces evil out of the evil

storeroom, for his mouth speaks from the overflow of the heart.

Luke 6:45

And since we have the same spirit of faith in accordance with what is written, I believed, therefore I spoke, we also believe, and therefore speak.

2 Corinthians 4:13

I assure you: If anyone says to this mountain, 'Be lifted up and thrown into the sea,' and does not doubt in his heart, but believes that what he says will happen, it will be done for him.

Mark 11:23

What the Bible says about…WISDOM
Now if any of you lacks wisdom, he should ask God, who gives to all generously and without criticizing, and it will be given to him. But let him ask in faith without doubting. For the doubter is like the surging sea, driven and tossed by the wind.

James 1:5-6

Get wisdom, get understanding; don't forget or turn away from the words of my mouth. Don't abandon wisdom, and she will watch over you; love her, and she will guard you. Wisdom is supreme—so get wisdom. And whatever else you get, get understanding.

Proverbs 4:5-7

My son, if you accept my words and store up my commands within you, listening closely to wisdom and directing your heart to understanding; then you will understand the fear of the Lord and discover the knowledge of God. For the Lord gives wisdom; from His mouth come knowledge and understanding.

Proverbs 2:1-2, 5-6

For where envy and selfish ambition exist, there is disorder and every kind of evil. But the wisdom from above is first pure, then peace-loving, gentle, compliant, full of mercy and good fruits, without favoritism and hypocrisy.

James 3:16-17

My speech and my proclamation were not with persuasive words of wisdom, but with a demonstration of the Spirit and power, so that your faith might not be based on men's wisdom but on God's power. However, among the mature we do speak a wisdom, but not a wisdom of this age, or of the rulers of this age, who are coming to nothing. On the contrary, we speak God's hidden wisdom in a mystery, which God predestined before the ages for our glory. None of the rulers of this age knew it, for if they had known it, they would not have crucified the Lord of glory.

1 Corinthians 2:4-8

Where is the philosopher? Where is the scholar? Where is the debater of this age? Hasn't God made the world's wisdom foolish? For since, in God's wisdom, the world did not know God through wisdom, God was pleased to save those who believe through the foolishness of the message preached.

1 Corinthians 1:20-21

What the Bible says about… WHO WE ARE IN CHRIST

Because whatever has been born of God conquers the world. This is the victory that has conquered the world: our faith.

1 John 5:4

For: who has known the Lord's mind, that he may instruct Him? But we have the mind of Christ.

1 Corinthians 2:16

May grace and peace be multiplied to you through the knowledge of God and of Jesus our Lord. For His divine power has given us everything required for life and godliness, through the knowledge of Him who called us by His own glory and goodness. By these He has given us very great and precious promises, so that through them you may share in the divine nature, escaping the corruption that is in the world because of evil desires.

2 Peter 1:2-4

You are from God, little children, and you have conquered them, because the One who is in you is greater than the one who is in the world.

1 John 4:4

Look, I have given you the authority to trample on snakes and scorpions and over all the power of the enemy; nothing will ever harm you.

Luke 10:19

Therefore if anyone is in Christ, there is a new creation; old things have passed away, and look, new things have come.

2 Corinthians 5:17

And if the Spirit of Him who raised Jesus from the dead lives in you, then He who raised Christ from the dead will also bring your mortal bodies to life through His Spirit who lives in you.

Romans 8:11

While He was together with them, He commanded them not to leave Jerusalem, but to wait for the Father's promise. "This," [He said, "is what] you heard from Me; for John baptized with water, but you will be baptized with the Holy Spirit not many days from now."

Acts 1:4-5

He is the Spirit of truth. The world is unable to receive Him because it doesn't see Him or know Him. But you do know Him, because He remains with you and will be in you. I will not leave you as orphans; I am coming to you. In a little while the world will see Me no longer, but you will see Me. Because I live, you will live too.

John 14:17-19

God wants you to...BE CONTENT
But godliness with contentment is a great gain. For we brought nothing into the world, and we can take

nothing out. But if we have food and clothing, we will be content with these. But those who want to be rich fall into temptation, a trap, and many foolish and harmful desires, which plunge people into ruin and destruction. For the love of money is a root of all kinds of evil, and by craving it, some have wandered away from the faith and pierced themselves with many pains.

1 Timothy 6:6-10

I know both how to have a little, and I know how to have a lot. In any and all circumstances I have learned the secret [of being content]—whether well-fed or hungry, whether in abundance or in need. I am able to do all things through Him who strengthens me.

Philippians 4:12-13

The Lord is my shepherd; there is nothing I lack. He lets me lie down in green pastures; He leads me beside quiet waters. He renews my life; He leads me along the right paths for His name's sake.

Psalm 23:1-3

Search me, God, and know my heart; test me and know my concerns. See if there is any offensive way in me; lead me in the everlasting way.

Psalm 139: 23-24

A joyful heart is good medicine, but a broken spirit dries up the bones.

Proverbs 17:22

Your life should be free from the love of money. Be satisfied with what you have, for He Himself has said, I will never leave you or forsake you.

Hebrews 13:5

All the days of the oppressed are miserable, but a cheerful heart has a continual feast.

Proverbs 15:15

A tranquil heart is life to the body, but jealousy is rottenness to the bones.

Proverbs 14:30

God wants you to…BE OBEDIENT
See, today I have set before you life and prosperity, death and adversity. For I am commanding you today to love the Lord your God, to walk in His ways, and to keep His commands, statutes, and ordinances, so that you may live and multiply, and the Lord your God may bless you in the land you are entering to possess.

Deuteronomy 30:15-16

If only they had such a heart to fear Me and keep all
My commands, so that they and their children will
prosper forever.

Deuteronomy 5:29

Therefore, observe the words of this covenant and
follow them, so that you will succeed in everything
you do.

Deuteronomy 29:9

Do what you have learned and received and heard and
seen in me, and the God of peace will be with you.

Philippians 4:9

"Therefore, everyone who hears these words of Mine
and acts on them will be like a sensible man who built
his house on the rock. The rain fell, the rivers rose, and
the winds blew and pounded that house. Yet it didn't
collapse, because its foundation was on the rock.

Matthew 7:24-25

But the one who looks intently into the perfect law
of freedom and perseveres in it, and is not a forgetful
hearer but a doer who acts—this person will be
blessed in what he does.

James 1:25

If you keep My commands you will remain in My love, just as I have kept My Father's commands and remain in His love.

John 15:10

Dear friends, if our hearts do not condemn [us] we have confidence before God, and can receive whatever we ask from Him because we keep His commands and do what is pleasing in His sight.

1 John 3:21-22

For the hearers of the law are not righteous before God, but the doers of the law will be declared righteous.

Romans 2:13

And the world with its lust is passing away, but the one who does God's will remains forever.

1 John 2:17

After He was perfected, He became the source of eternal salvation to all who obey Him.

Hebrews 5:9

God wants you to…BE PATIENT

Therefore, brothers, be patient until the Lord's coming. See how the farmer waits for the precious fruit of the earth and is patient with it until it receives the early and the late rains. You also must be patient. Strengthen your hearts, because the Lord's coming is near.

James 5:7-8

So we must not get tired of doing good, for we will reap at the proper time if we don't give up.

Galatians 6:9

Now we want each of you to demonstrate the same diligence for the final realization of your hope, so that you won't become lazy, but imitators of those who inherit the promises through faith and perseverance.

Hebrews 6:11-12

So don't throw away your confidence, which has a great reward. For you need endurance, so that after you have done God's will, you may receive what was promised.

Hebrews 10:35-36

Consider it a great joy, my brothers, whenever you experience various trials, knowing that the testing of your faith produces endurance. But endurance must do its complete work, so that you may be mature and complete, lacking nothing.

James 1:2-4

And not only that, but we also rejoice in our afflictions, because we know that affliction produces endurance, endurance produces proven character, and proven character produces hope.

Romans 5: 3-4

But the fruit of the Spirit is love, joy, peace, patience, kindness, goodness, faith, gentleness, self-control. Against such things there is no law.

Galatians 5:22-23

But those who trust in the Lord will renew their strength; they will soar on wings like eagles; they will run and not grow weary; they will walk and not faint.

Isaiah 40:31

Wait for the Lord; be courageous and let your heart be strong. Wait for the Lord.

Psalm 27:14

It is good to wait quietly for deliverance from the Lord.

Lamentations 3:26

But if we hope for what we do not see, we eagerly wait for it with patience.

Romans 8:25

God wants you to…GIVE

Give, and it will be given to you; a good measure—pressed down, shaken together, and running over—will be poured into your lap. For with the measure you use, it will be measured back to you."

Luke 6:38

Each person should do as he has decided in his heart—not out of regret or out of necessity, for God loves a cheerful giver.

2 Corinthians 9:7

"Bring the full 10 percent into the storehouse so that there may be food in My house. Test Me in this way," says the Lord of Hosts. "See if I will not open the floodgates of heaven and pour out a blessing for you without measure."

Malachi 3:10

Kindness to the poor is a loan to the Lord, and He will give a reward to the lender.

Proverbs 19:17

A generous person will be blessed, for he shares his food with the poor.

Proverbs 22:9

The one who gives to the poor will not be in need, but one who turns his eyes away will receive many curses.

Proverbs 28:27

One person gives freely, yet gains more; another withholds what is right, only to become poor. A generous person will be enriched, and the one who gives a drink of water will receive water.

Proverbs 11:24-25

Instruct those who are rich in the present age not to be arrogant or to set their hope on the uncertainty of wealth, but on God, who richly provides us with all things to enjoy. [Instruct them] to do good, to be rich in good works, to be generous, willing to share, storing up for themselves a good foundation for the age to come, so that they may take hold of life that is real.

1 Timothy 6:17-19

But when you give to the poor, don't let your left
hand know what your right hand is doing, so that
your giving may be in secret. And your Father who
sees in secret will reward you.

Matthew 6:3-4

God wants you to...PRAY
Don't worry about anything, but in everything,
through prayer and petition with thanksgiving, let
your requests be made known to God. And the peace
of God, which surpasses every thought, will guard
your hearts and your minds in Christ Jesus.

Philippians 4:6-7

Rejoice always! Pray constantly. Give thanks in
everything, for this is God's will for you in Christ Jesus.

1 Thessalonians 5:16-18

If you remain in Me and My words remain in you,
ask whatever you want and it will be done for you.

John 15:7

But when you pray, go into your private room, shut
your door, and pray to your Father who is in secret.
And your Father who sees in secret will reward you.

Matthew 6:6

Therefore let us approach the throne of grace with boldness, so that we may receive mercy and find grace to help us at the proper time.

Hebrews 4:16

Therefore, confess your sins to one another and pray for one another, so that you may be healed. The intense prayer of the righteous is very powerful.

James 5:16

Again, I assure you: If two of you on earth agree about any matter that you pray for, it will be done for you by My Father in heaven. For where two or three are gathered together in My name, I am there among them.

Matthew 18:19-20

Even before they call, I will answer; while they are still speaking, I will hear.

Isaiah 65:24

Whatever you ask in My name, I will do it so that the Father may be glorified in the Son.

John 14:13

When he calls out to Me, I will answer him; I will be with him in trouble. I will rescue him and give him honor. I will satisfy him with a long life and show him My salvation.

Psalm 91:15-16

Call to Me and I will answer you and tell you great and wondrous things you do not know.

Jeremiah 33:3

First of all, then, I urge that petitions, prayers, intercessions, and thanksgivings be made for everyone, for kings and all those who are in authority, so that we may lead a tranquil and quiet life in all godliness and dignity.

1 Timothy 2:1-2

God wants you to…PROSPER
A thief comes only to steal and to kill and to destroy. I have come that they may have life and have it in abundance.

John 10:10

Who is the person who fears the Lord? He will show him the way he should choose. He will live a good life, and his descendants will inherit the land.

Psalm 25:12-13

Give, and it will be given to you; a good measure—
pressed down, shaken together, and running over—
will be poured into your lap. For with the measure
you use, it will be measured back to you.

Luke 6:38

A man's steps are established by the Lord, and He
takes pleasure in his way. Though he falls, he will
not be overwhelmed, because the Lord holds his
hand. I have been young and now I am old, yet I
have not seen the righteous abandoned or his children
begging bread.

Psalm 37:23-25

All these blessings will come and overtake you,
because you obey the Lord your God: You will be
blessed in the city and blessed in the country. Your
descendants will be blessed, and your soil's produce,
and the offspring of your livestock, including the young
of your herds and the newborn of your flocks. Your
basket and kneading bowl will be blessed. You will
be blessed when you come in and blessed when you
go out. "The Lord will cause the enemies who rise
up against you to be defeated before you. They will
march out against you from one direction but flee
from you in seven directions. The Lord will grant

you a blessing on your storehouses and on everything
you do; He will bless you in the land the Lord your
God is giving you.

Deuteronomy 28:2-8

But seek first the kingdom of God and His righteousness,
and all these things will be provided for you.

Matthew 6:33

Dear friend, I pray that you may prosper in every way
and be in good health, just as your soul prospers.

3 John 2

God wants you to…SHARE YOUR FAITH
Then Jesus came near and said to them, "All authority
has been given to Me in heaven and on earth. Go,
therefore, and make disciples of all nations, baptizing
them in the name of the Father and of the Son and of
the Holy Spirit, teaching them to observe everything
I have commanded you. And remember, I am with
you always, to the end of the age."

Matthew 28:18-20

You are the light of the world. A city situated on a hill
cannot be hidden. No one lights a lamp and puts it

under a basket, but rather on a lampstand, and it gives light for all who are in the house. In the same way, let your light shine before men, so that they may see your good works and give glory to your Father in heaven.

Matthew 5:14-16

But how can they call on Him in whom they have not believed? And how can they believe without hearing about Him? And how can they hear without a preacher? And how can they preach unless they are sent? As it is written: How welcome are the feet of those who announce the gospel of good things!

Romans 10:14-15

What I tell you in the dark, speak in the light. What you hear in a whisper, proclaim on the housetops.

Matthew 10:27

As He was getting into the boat, the man who had been demon-possessed kept begging Him to be with Him. But He would not let him; instead, He told him, "Go back home to your own people, and report to them how much the Lord has done for you and how He has had mercy on you." So he went out and began to proclaim in the Decapolis how much Jesus had done for him, and they were all amazed.

Mark 5:18-20

Then He said to them, "Go into all the world and preach the gospel to the whole creation. Whoever believes and is baptized will be saved, but whoever does not believe will be condemned."

Mark 16:15-16

He also said to them, "This is what is written: the Messiah would suffer and rise from the dead the third day, and repentance for forgiveness of sins would be proclaimed in His name to all the nations, beginning at Jerusalem."

Luke 24:46-47

This good news of the kingdom will be proclaimed in all the world as a testimony to all nations. And then the end will come.

Matthew 24:14

God wants you to…UTILIZE YOUR TALENT
Whatever you do, do it enthusiastically, as something done for the Lord and not for men, knowing that you will receive the reward of an inheritance from the Lord—you serve the Lord Christ.

Colossians 3:23-24

Therefore, I remind you to keep ablaze the gift of God that is in you through the laying on of my hands. For God has not given us a spirit of fearfulness, but one of power, love, and sound judgment.

2 Timothy 1:6-7

You are the light of the world. A city situated on a hill cannot be hidden. No one lights a lamp and puts it under a basket, but rather on a lampstand, and it gives light for all who are in the house. In the same way, let your light shine before men, so that they may see your good works and give glory to your Father in heaven.

Matthew 5:14-16

I assure you: The one who believes in Me will also do the works that I do. And he will do even greater works than these, because I am going to the Father.

John 14:12

...since God's gracious gifts and calling are irrevocable.

Romans 11:29

For as we have many members in one body, but all the members do not have the same function, so we, being many, are one body in Christ, and individually members of one another. Having then gifts differing according to the grace that is given to us, let us use them.

Romans 12:4-6 (NKJV)

For just as the body without the spirit is dead, so also faith without works is dead.

James 2:26

A man's gift makes room for him, and brings him before great men.

Proverbs 18:16 (NKJV)

And how can they preach unless they are sent? As it is written: How welcome are the feet of those who announce the gospel of good things!

Romans 10:15

The man who had received five talents approached, presented five more talents, and said, "Master, you gave me five talents. Look, I've earned five more talents." His master said to him, "Well done, good and faithful slave! You were faithful over a few things; I will put you in charge of many things. Share your master's joy!"

Matthew 25:20-21

God wants you to...WORSHIP HIM

But an hour is coming, and is now here, when the true worshipers will worship the Father in spirit and truth. Yes, the Father wants such people to worship Him. God is spirit, and those who worship Him must worship in spirit and truth."

John 4:23-24

All the earth will worship You and sing praise to You. They will sing praise to Your name.

Psalms 66:4

The trumpeters and singers joined together to praise and thank the Lord with one voice. They raised [their] voices, accompanied by trumpets, cymbals, and musical instruments, in praise to the Lord: For He is good; His faithful love endures forever; the temple, the Lord's temple, was filled with a cloud. And because of the cloud, the priests were not able to continue ministering, for the glory of the Lord filled God's temple.

2 Chronicles 5:13-14

Stand up. Bless the Lord your God from everlasting to everlasting. Praise Your glorious name, and may it be exalted above all blessing and praise. You alone are the Lord. You created the heavens, the highest

All the ends of the earth will remember and turn to the Lord. All the families of the nations will bow down before You, for kingship belongs to the Lord; He rules over the nations.

Psalm 22:27-28

Give the Lord—you heavenly beings—give the Lord glory and strength. Give the Lord the glory due His name; worship the Lord in the splendor of [His] holiness.

Psalms 29:1-2

All the nations You have made will come and bow down before You, Lord, and will honor Your name.

Psalms 86:9

Come, let us shout joyfully to the Lord, shout triumphantly to the rock of our salvation! Let us enter His presence with thanksgiving; let us shout triumphantly to Him in song.

Psalms 95:1-2

Come, let us worship and bow down; let us kneel before the Lord our Maker. For He is our God, and we are the people of His pasture, the sheep under His care.

Psalms 95:6-7

Exalt the Lord our God; bow in worship at His footstool.

Psalms 99:5

Study notes written by Stan Moser
Scriptures compiled by Sue Moser
Cover design by Ben Arrowood for Right Hand Design

About the authors:

Stan Moser has been a leading executive in the Christian music industry for over 30 years, helping to build a number of music companies including Word Records & Music, Maranatha!Music, StarSong Communications, and Ministry Music. He has worked closely with those who write and record the songs that the church has grown to love, including Bill Gaither, Twila Paris, Ralph Carmichael, Andrae Crouch, Evie, The Imperials, Amy Grant, Terry MacAlmon, and many more. He currently serves a variety of worship ministries as a consultant, and continues to be active in the Christian music industry.

Sue Moser began her career at Family Life Communications in Tucson, Arizona. She served there as a producer and engineer for the highly acclaimed radio program, Parent Talk, with Dr. Randy Carlson and Dr. Kevin Leman. Sue currently serves as editor of SingersClub.com, manages Songtracks.com, and coordinates worship events for Terry MacAlmon Ministries. Stan and Sue founded Music And The Word Ministries in 2001.

Music And The Word Ministries is a not for profit ministry dedicated to teaching biblical purpose for Christian singers, musicians, and worship leaders.

Great and Precious Promises for Singers and Musicians makes an ideal gift for anyone who desires to sing and play for the Lord.

<u>Worship Leaders</u>—a perfect gift for every member of your team.

<u>Ministers of Music</u>—every choir member can learn to release their potential and fulfill their purpose.

<u>Singers and Musicians</u>—every Scripture has been carefully selected to meet singers and musicians at their point of need.

Other valuable websites for singers and musicians:
<u>www.singersclub.com</u> For great articles and demos of the latest accompaniment tracks.
<u>www.songtracks.com</u> A great source for accompaniment tracks and free postage.

Music And The Word Ministries
419 Dahlia Drive
Brentwood, TN 37027
(615) 221-5111
<u>www.musicandtheword.com</u>